7 Effective Steps To Transform A Messy Teenager

How To Improve Your Teen's Organizational Skills

Jessica L. Stevenson

indirect, that are incurred as a result of the use of the information contained within this document, including, but not limited to, errors, omissions, or inaccuracies.

Table of Contents

Introduction

Raising teens is no easy feat. When your once bright, bubbly, sticky-fingered, sleepy little kiddo reaches the infamous teen years, it can feel like your whole world has been turned upside down. Playful afternoons filled with coloring and dancing are turned to dreadful evening arguments about messy rooms and missing belongings.

As much as we love our children, their teenage years can be among some of the most challenging. It's difficult when you've asked them to keep their room tidy and yet, once again, you can't open the door wide enough to get inside and exterminate the strange odors wafting out from under their door. It's frustrating when you feel as though you're asking them time and again to clean up, and all you hear is "I'll do it later."

Mysteriously, later never comes.

Then, when that dreadful moment comes that they've misplaced something important to them, it's like World War III has broken out in your home. Teenagers have a tendency to lose their minds, frantically searching for said item. Meanwhile, you're frustrated because had they just put it away and taken care of their stuff *like you already told them,* none of you would be in this mess. Of course, your teenager never slows down long enough to acknowledge that or take responsibility for their role in this occurrence.

As much as they long to be independent little adults, they still operate heavily on the emotional and self-centered mindset of their youth. And while it is easy to get trapped in these back-and-forth cycles with them over what's what, that rarely brings any family to a meaningful solution.

Wouldn't it be nice if you have a clear, step-by-step plan to help your teenager get (and stay) organized, and to help *you* have a more peaceful home? That's what *7 Effective Steps To Transform A Messy Teenager* is all about!

This book will show you:

- How to evaluate and create a common objective with your teenager
- The value of setting targets and routines to create consistency that leads to excellent organizational skills and abilities
- How to help your teenager differentiate between wants and needs and prioritize their time and efforts accordingly
- Habits that will help your teenager maintain optimal health so their energy levels and wellbeing don't impede their ability to stay focused
- Improving your teen's organizational skills by assigning them various roles and give them a chance to practice their skills
- The purpose of long-term goals and dreams, and how to motivate your teenager to develop theirs

I know you don't want to wait around and hear about how great this transformation will be – you want to get right into it! So, without further   ado,   let's   go!

Step 1

Start with A Simple Checklist

Organizational skills are an asset to a healthy life, and teenagers are at the perfect age to begin learning about them. As children, their organizational expectations were fairly simple: keep your room clean. As our children grow into teenagers, though, life begins to place more demands on them.

They have homework deadlines to maintain, social gatherings to factor in, big life choices looming on the horizon, and far more responsibility by way of maintaining their personal health. Knowing how to organize their time, energy, resources, and attention effectively helps teenagers keep on top of everything.

Of course, it is to be expected that teenagers are going to make mistakes. We all do. Teenagers are likely to make *more* mistakes when it comes to organizing their time, energy, and efforts, because they're still learning about the value of priorities, wants vs. needs, and time itself. Regardless, helping your teenager understand the basics and develop organizational skills and systems ensures that any time they make a mistake, they understand *why* it was a mistake, and they have a good idea of how to correct it. Offering this level of support to your teenager increases their autonomy and gives them a chance to practice for adulthood.

The first step to helping your teenager develop their organization skills is developing a system that shows them how to get organized in the first place. If your house has been particularly chaotic, keeping your earliest steps as simple as possible will prevent both you and your teenager from becoming overwhelmed. This will also help you begin to identify larger problem areas that need more attention.

A good starting point is to help your teenager organize his or her time for just one day. In other words, sit down together and look at all the things they need to do the following day. Factor in everything they need to do for home, school, and work, as well as anything they may want to do such as spending time with friends or going somewhere for leisure. Once you have a list of everything that needs to get done, organize that list around their typical day to day structure: morning, school, after school, dinner time, evening, and bedtime.

Next, turn their activities into a checklist. Once everything is organized, all that's left to do is start the day! Chances are, by the time they get to the end of the day, they could at least have completed half of what have been scheduled on their checklist.

If you notice your teen resisting the checklist or struggling to stay on track with it, this would be a good time to check in and ask why. Getting their feedback on what your teenager feels they need more of in their life, or day, to stay organized will help you modify any of these steps to match your teenagers' needs. At the end of the day, creating a custom system that works for your teenager is more important than trying to force your teenager to stay on track with someone else's plan. This way, they are more likely to see it through, and it's more likely to have results.

At this point, you can sit down together and create another one for the following day, taking into account of any adjustments or finetuning. You should do this task together for several days in a row, until you begin to notice a pattern in your teenagers' life. When your teenager begins to feel confident in this process, they can start making their own checklists so they feel more personal control over how they're spending their time.

Tip: If your teenager struggles to stay on track with their checklist, consider programming it into the note app on their smartphone so they can keep the list with them. That way, they can't make the excuse that they left it at home.

You might also program a few reminders into your own phone, so you can check in with them to see how they're doing, and to offer any help if they need it.

Step 2

Setting Targets and Routines

Setting up an effective checklist is a great starting point for your teenager, which is the first step towards a successful long-term goal. Having established a pattern of your teenager's daily schedule, you should create routines for the morning, after school, and before bed.

Keeping routines broken up in this way benefits your teenager by giving them a chance to reset between one routine to the next. This benefits your teenager in two ways: by offering three chances (instead of one) to succeed at new tasks each day, which boosts their confidence, and by offering them a chance to try again any time they miss a routine. As well, they are more likely to pay attention because their routines aren't all-consuming, instead they're focused on "hot spots" throughout their day.

For example, if your teenager tends to rush around in the morning and it causes them to forget to take their homework or lunch to school, and also causes them to be angry and stressed, it would be a good idea to address this. Choosing an earlier wake time and allocating sufficient time around every task —so your teenager is able to get everything done, including eating breakfast, packing a lunch, getting ready, and gathering their belongings—will help them have a better morning routine. It will also help you experience more peace, as you won't have a chaotic teenager storming about the house each morning and then heading off to have an inevitably stressful day at school.

Routines are a powerful way to help your teenager get into the habit of working toward their goals. They provide the much-needed stability that would guide your child to think and act rationally with a calm mindset. Strong routines take into account both your teenager's natural tendencies, and their greatest needs. Targets, or milestones, help them know when they're making positive progress toward them. These targets are excellent for boosting your teen's confidence, as well, as they genuinely feel good when they realize they're moving in a positive direction in life.

As you create your teenager's new routine together, make sure you write it down. This will help them recall each step as they get into the habit of executing that routine, and will ensure they don't miss any important steps. Make sure you keep the written copy of their routine somewhere visible (Igo, 2020).

The biggest challenge you are likely to face with your teenager is laziness when it comes to executing their new routine. Often, when we have done something the same way for so long, it can take time to adapt to a new process. Helping your teenager create consistent triggers to signify the start of a routine, such as an alarm clock or coming home from school, will help them stay on track. You may also celebrate their milestones by recognizing their effort and celebrating them for staying on-track. This is a great way to boost their confidence and help your teenager stay focused on fulfilling their routines.

Don't Forget*: Teenagers, like anyone else, are prone to having off-days. This means they are likely to have days* *where they simply don't see their routines through. It can be helpful to have a rule where if they don't see their routines through one day, they immediately jump back on track the next day without missing milestone celebrations. This way, they don't use excuses for why they stopped, and why they can't get back on track.*

Step 3

Prioritizing Needs VS. Wants

Teenagers are infamous for having a massive struggle between "wants" versus "needs." This is because teens are still largely externally motivated, and haven't learned the power of intrinsic motivation (Uche, 2018).

This means they are heavily influenced by their peers, culture, social media, and the world around them in general. Anytime they see something that stirs feelings of curiosity, jealousy, or desire, they're more likely to prioritize them over things that are actually important to your teen's wellbeing.

Naturally, you don't want your teenager making the mistake of prioritizing desires over needs, because it leads to long-term issues. Your teenager begins to struggle with simple tasks like hygiene, time management, and finishing school tasks, because they're busy focusing on following their desires. In the end, they end up dealing with ill health, last minute "emergencies" that cause them to be unable to follow through on their responsibilities, and poor grades. Which, inevitably, causes more troubles for them, thus creating a negative spiral of stress and poor relationships at home.

The best way to teach the difference of wants versus needs, aside from regular conversation, is to teach the choice-consequence connection to your teenager. Teenagers need to feel "free" to make their own choices, but they should not be shielded by their parents when the consequences come along (Pickhardt,2018). For example, if your teenager chooses to prioritize friends over homework and gets a failing grade in school, then they face the consequence of being grounded for that failing grade. In this scenario, they learn about natural consequences, and will begin to personally understand why they need to make stronger decisions.

As a parent in these scenarios, the best thing you can do is be honest with your teenager and explain to them why their decision was wrong and why they need to do better. It can be easy for parents to want to swoop in and lessen the hardship their teenager faces by minimizing the seriousness of consequences, or preventing consequences altogether. Being honest with your teenager about things, such as poor grades being a bad outcome, enables them to sit with their consequences and truly begin to understand why we need to avoid them by being responsible.

You can also help your teenager by teaching them to use the choice-consequence connection with prediction. In other words, as your teenager begins to accumulate evidence of the connection, teach them to start asking themselves the question of "If I made this choice, what consequences are likely to occur?" This way, they can think their choices through and make them responsibly.

It is especially important to explain to your teenager the need for such a question during exciting moments, such as ones where peers are enthusiastically encouraging your teenager to make a poor choice. If your teenager is being pressured to go home late, or skip school, for example, this is a great time to ask the question and realize that no, the consequences are not worth the few minutes of fun they might experience if they take that action.

The biggest challenge you are likely to face with this step is your teenager not realizing the significance of consequences, and struggling to realize when consequences are not worth it. Often, it takes a few bad experiences for a teenager to realize that consequences are real, and they're not enjoyable. As they start to build some life experience, your teenager will begin to realize the reality of consequences, and will be able to predict consequences and avoid making choices that would lead to even stronger, and possibly more severe consequences.

Note*: Avoid layering on consequences, or adding consequences that make no sense to the choice your teenager has made. For example, if your teenager doesn't do their homework, a natural consequence would be that they no longer get to choose when to do their homework because you're going to decide that for them. A poor consequence would be that they're grounded from the TV for a week, but can still go about doing whatever else they want. In the former, you're teaching the priority of homework, and in the latter, it just comes across as you being unfair.*

Step 4

Creating Healthy Habits & Building Resiliency

Despite what you may realize, your teenager already has a plethora of habits built around their day-to-day life. By definition, habits don't change. There may be slight variations, but the habits themselves are always the same (O'Keefe, 2022).

With that being said, we can break habits and build new ones, if we're willing to put the effort in.

Since habits account for about 40% of our daily behaviors, it makes sense that your teenagers need strong, healthy habits that assist them in making good choices. At their young age, this is the perfect time to set up healthy habits. The longer these healthy habits are reinforced, the stronger they will become, and the better your teenager will be at following through with them long-term.

The best way to help your teenager build healthier habits is to talk to them and have them help you identify the problems they're facing as a result of their current habits. Then, you can get their input on why they think they're having such problems, and what could be done to avoid having those problems continue in the future.

As you have this conversation, help your teenager identify the trigger, action, and reward their habits are offering them. This information will help you identify how to shift their habits so that the trigger and reward are more or less the same, but the habit is healthier in nature. For example, let's say your teenager comes home and turns on the TV because they want to relax, but you realize they're watching too much TV and it's causing them to skip doing homework or studying. In this case, coming home from school is the trigger, watching TV is the action, and feeling relaxed is the reward. Your goal is to either help your teenager find a new and equally satisfying action, or adjust their action so it's more beneficial. In this case, they might set a timer on the TV or an alarm on their phone so they know when to stop watching TV and start studying or doing their homework.

Aside from initiating the conversation and being a sounding board, your only role at this point is to listen and allow them to lead the conversation. You might be surprised to realize how committed your teenager is to doing better, especially now that you've been regularly having these conversations and working toward more organization in your lives as a family.

There is one additional, essential role you play as their parent that is more "walk-the-talk" in nature. That is, you are responsible for demonstrating healthy habits and improving on yourself on a regular basis. This way, your teenager sees you modeling the habits and behaviors you want them to have, and they're more likely to follow through in doing it for themselves, too. This may seem like "behind the scenes work" – and it is – but it is crucial, as it allows your teenager to *see* how good, healthy habits look in practice.

When it comes to helping teenagers build healthy habits, one of the biggest challenges you're likely to face is having them break their bad habits. Breaking bad habits is difficult for anyone, but may be even more difficult for teenagers who don't have a deep sense of meaning behind *why* their bad habits need to be broken, and healthy habits need to be followed. This is where the choice-consequence connection can be used to teach your teenager the value of good habits, good behavior, and good follow through.

Reminder: *If your teenager is struggling to set and follow healthy habits, make sure they're being realistic with themselves about what they can achieve. Setting one habit at a time and working toward fulfilling that habit, until it becomes a true habit, and then setting another one may be better than trying to set too many new habits at once.*

Step 5

Putting Their Skills to Work

Not too long ago, your teenager was a child and their role in the home was fairly small. They were too young to help out with organizational and administration tasks related to family life, so they were more focused on playing and enjoying themselves.

As they grow into young adults, teenagers may staunchly resist taking on more responsibility and chores, but the reality is that they need them.

Having a sense of responsibility that contributes to the wellbeing of the family gives your teenager the opportunity to feel a sense of purpose in their lives. They begin to realize how meaningful they are, how much value their efforts add to the lives of others, and why they need to be actively participating in building up the world around them.

One day, your teenager will have their own home to organize and manage, and they will need to use these skills elsewhere such as in their careers and communities, too. Helping your teenager develop a sense of purpose and meaning now means when they grow up and move away, they'll have the skills needed to organize their time, energy, and resources in their own homes, workplaces, and communities.

Before your teenager is ready to launch into all those larger initiatives, they need to start at home. Giving your teenager responsibilities such as cleaning up or reorganizing the garage, organizing the food pantry, managing the weekly shopping list, or organizing the family calendar is a great way to help them put their organizational skills to good use. Each of these tasks helps your teenager expand their thinking skills and organize things in a way that makes sense and supports the greater purpose of that tool.

Simple organizational skills such as how and where to organize your belongings is a task most adults take for granted. Often, we've been organizing our own spaces for so long that it seems like common sense to keep common use items nearby, and items we only use from time to time in the more difficult-to-reach spots. For teenagers, though, this is not common sense until they have had to deal with the frustration of reaching to those harder-to-reach areas several times over. Then, they discover the value of organizing their space in such a way that prioritizes high use items.

For example, tasking your teenager with organizing the pantry requires them to think about which items are likely to be used together and, therefore, which items should be grouped together in the pantry. It also helps them understand the value of making frequently used items more easily accessible, and putting lesser used items in harder to reach spaces. This way, their everyday tasks like pouring breakfast cereal are made easier through accessibility.

Nearly every household task your teenager can assist with will help them begin to understand the importance of priority-based organizational skills. The more you let your teenager practice these skills, the stronger their organization will be, and the less stressed they will be in the long-run.

Understand that while these skills are certainly age-appropriate, chances are your teenager will push back. They will complain about taking on responsibility, suggest it's unfair that they have to clean the garage or the pantry, or otherwise try to get out of doing these tasks. It may be easy to want to give in, but in doing so, you take away an opportunity for them to learn about important organizational skills. It's better to endure the complaints but require they see it through, than to give in and let them get out of their responsibilities. In doing the latter, all you teach your teenager is that they can pass responsibility along to someone else, which won't serve them at all when they are adults and there is no one else to pass the responsibility on to.

Tip: If your teenager seems overwhelmed with a new responsibility, coach them through it. Explain the steps to them, and give them tips on how to do a good job. Then, step back and let them figure it out for themselves.

Step 6

Cultivating Long-Term Goals with A Sense of Purpose

Teenagers may be relatively inexperienced with life, but they still have a strong need for dreams and long-term goals. Further, many already have a strong idea of what they want to do with their life, though they may be reluctant to talk about it for fear of being judged.

Helping your teenager feel confident in his or her long-term goals is a great way to help them cultivate those goals and use them as a way to give themselves a sense of direction. With a clear focus on where they're going, they can base all their choices off these goals. For many teenagers, this is key in keeping them out of trouble because they realize their efforts on each individual task are building toward something bigger.

As a parent, it is essential to make it clear that cultivating dreams and long-term goals is not a permanent commitment. Teenagers are often pressured with this notion that they should have their entire lives figured out by a young age, when in reality, even most adults don't have that much clarity about their lives. Relieving that pressure and ensuring that your teenager knows that you are only focusing on present interests, dreams, and goals may help them be more involved in cultivating dreams and development long-term goals in the first place.

Giving your teenager the flexibility to move toward something they care about, while also being able to change their mind and focus elsewhere if they discover they would like to try something else is important. In fact, you can even build this flexibility into the foundation of their dreams if you use the SMART goal method.

According to *A Beginner's Guide to Goal Setting for Teens* (2020), SMART goals help your teenager clearly define their goals and stay focused on working toward something bigger than themselves. They are also built in such a way that your teenager can reevaluate their goals and keep them focused to their truest desires through simple shifts and readjustments over time.

To help your teenager make a SMART goal, you're going to assist them with fitting their long-term goals to this outline:

Specific: The goal defines exactly what your teenager will accomplish.

Measurable: There are clear milestones so your teenager can track their progress.

Achievable: It would be reasonable for your teenager to achieve this goal.

Relevant: The outcome of the goal is aligned with what your teenager desires.

Timely: The goal includes fair, but firm, deadlines.

It is within the milestones and deadlines that you have the opportunity to "review the goal" and "ensure it still matches your teenagers' desires." In other words, you may decide with your teenager that every month, other month, or even every third month you will both check-in and see how they feel about their current long-term goals. If they decide at that point that the goal is no longer aligned with what they desire for themselves, then you can adjust as needed.

If you attempt this exercise and your teenager genuinely seems to have no sense of direction, you can help your teenager by keeping track of what interests them, and what would allow them to feel good in their current lives (Help Unmotivated Teen Develop Long-Term Goals, 2016). For example, if your teenager is presently interested in sports, you might discover that they would be happiest pursuing a scholarship based on their chosen sport. Or, if your teenager is particularly fascinated with animal welfare, you might discover that they would be happiest volunteering at a vet clinic or an animal shelter.

Helping your teenager discover their long-term dreams and align them with their personal interests is a great way to help them discover how to work toward something meaningful in life. It also gives them another chance to practice organizational skills, by organizing necessary tasks into their existing schedules and ensuring they have time to get everything done. This is an excellent way to practice time management, as well as resource management if they have to pay for their own uniform, transportation fees, or anything else related to their bigger goal.

At this point, you may discover that the biggest challenge you face with your teenager is one who seems unmotivated by the future. If this is the case, helping your teenager build a long-term vision that looks at the next 2-3 months for now is an excellent start. You can use that momentum to begin building 6-month goals, 12-month goals, and eventually goals that stretch beyond graduation.

Remember*: Teenagers are likely to change their mind around their long-term goals as they discover new interests or follow social trends alongside their friends. Adolescence is a perfect time to explore different opportunities, so don't resist this process. If, however, your teenager seems to be changing their mind every time something gets difficult, this would be a good opportunity to help them manage their expectations and create a plan to overcome their tendency toward giving up on things prematurely.*

Step 7

The Value of Rest and Good Health

High quality rest and good health are essential to anyone's wellbeing, and teenagers are no exemption. Often, teenagers are known for staying up late, eating junk food, and not taking great care of their bodies.

While this may be a tendency, it only lingers if the teenager is not taught proper self-care and health practices. It is essential that you teach your teenager about the value of rest and good health, and that you demonstrate habits and routines related to getting good rest and maintaining good health in your life, too.

Allowing your teenager to stay in a funk with their rest and health will directly impact their ability to remain organized, as they will succumb to great deals of stress in their life. They may find they are too exhausted to get up on time for school, too hungry to focus at school, or too restless to behave kindly around their family and peers. Knowing how to maintain rest and health will ensure that their body is working *for* them, not *against* them.

Research shows that we should focus on helping our teenagers maintain their health in four categories: physical, mental, emotional, and behavioral (Rippey, 2022). As a parent, you can help your teen identify and maintain these areas of good health through healthy habits. It is also worthwhile to have clear rules in your household, and consequences for what will happen if these rules are not followed. That way, your teenager is taught the value of good health *and* understand there are consequences for not maintaining good health.

Developing rules and routines around healthy eating, regular bedtimes and waketimes, and frequent exercise is important. Ideally, your teen should be involved in at least one physical activity as a part of their recreational activities, and should engage in regular movement through walking, swimming, biking, or any other aerobic activity.

Another area of health that should be focused on, especially relating to rest, isn't just about sleep but about mental and emotional rest, too. Teenagers often face a variety of mental and emotional stressors, ranging from pressures at school and in society, to overburdened schedules and expectations from parents and other authorities in their lives. It is important that, as their parent, you help your teenager manage this in a meaningful way.

The best way to help your teenager, aside from having rules and guidelines in your home, is to demonstrate healthy living to them. Show them how to politely say "no" and keep their schedules reasonable, even if it means letting someone else down because they are unable to complete more tasks than they have already committed to. Turn off your screens and have screen-free time where you relax and read a book, pray, meditate, or otherwise engage in some quiet time without loads of input coming in from every which angle. Eat healthy, and avoid excessively snacking on junk foods or convenience foods. The more you demonstrate healthy living for your teenager, the more likely they will recognize that it is a natural and important way of life and live that way themselves.

The biggest challenge you are likely to face in this area of helping your teenager get organized is them believing it is not as important as it is. Because of how their bodies are built, teenagers usually bounce back from physical ailments quickly. They also lack the self-awareness to realize that their poor mood and disorganization are likely directly related to poor health choices. Having regular conversations, and pointing these connections out, is a great way to help your teen develop this self-awareness and take their health seriously. Over time, they are likely to take it more and more seriously and make stronger and better decisions for themselves.

Tip: *If your teenager does not normally take good care of their health, and has not had much demonstration in this area of their life, chances are they're going to need extra help in cultivating healthy habits to support these meaningful shifts. It is important that you don't get angry or give up on your teen, as they need you now more than ever to show them why good health matters, and how they can have good health.*

Conclusion

Helping teenagers become more organized isn't about helping them buy cute folders and calendars and nagging them to make use of these tools. As most of us have already learned, teenagers won't listen to nagging anyway. If they do, it won't be for the value of learning a new skill, but to get us to be quiet.

Teaching your teenager the value of organization is an imperative life skill that will help them mitigate stress and overwhelm in the future, and live productive, functional lives. This means they need to understand how these skills work *and* why they are so valuable. While they may not fully grasp the value yet, they will begin to over time.

At their tender age, teenagers are already feeling pressured to pick a life path, be productive, and add value to society. While these are important milestones, teenagers are still learning and need a chance to figure it all out. Never underestimate the value of a well-intended parent showing them the ropes. Doing so will help them navigate current pressures, and prepare for the added pressures adulthood brings.

Don't feel discouraged if your child failed to accomplish all the 7 steps as mentioned in the book. Bear in mind that different kids develop these skills at a different pace (Lee, n.d.). Some teens could take into their mid-20s to develop such skills, since the prefrontal brain systems (which are pivotal in the development of executive or organization skills) are among one of the last to develop within the human brain (Meldrum, 2020). In fact, you should feel proud of your teen even if they managed to achieve just one of the many steps.

Lastly, if your teenager seems to struggle deeply with organizational skills, it's not unreasonable to recruit professional help. Therapists, coaches, and mentors are all excellent resources to tap into to help you gain an extra set of hands in the process of helping your teenager learn how to organize their lives and stay on top of their priorities.

I hope that reading *7 Effective Steps To Transform A Messy Teenager* supported your understanding of your teenager's needs, why your teenager likely resists your efforts, and how you can help them in a way that they understand and value.

Finally, if you enjoyed reading this book, I ask that you please take the time to review it on your favorite retailer. Your honest feedback would be appreciated, as it helps me write more titles that will serve you and your family through your precious periods of growth. Thank you!

***

Resources

Igo, R. (2020). How to Help Your Teen Create a Successful Daily Routine. Outward Bound. *https://www.outwardbound.org/blog/how-to-help-your-teen-create-a-successful-daily-routine/*

Uche, U. (2018). Why Your Teen Struggles with Motivation. Psychology Today. *https://www.psychologytoday.com/ca/blog/promoting-empathy-your-teen/201807/why-your-teen-struggles-motivation*

Pickhardt, C.E., Ph.D. (2018.) Parenting Adolescents and the Choice-Consequence Connection. Psychology Today. *https://www.psychologytoday.com/ca/blog/surviving-your-childs-adolescence/201809/parenting-adolescents-and-the-choice-consequence*

O'Keefe, K. (2022). Good Habits, Good Life: How to Start Good Habits with Your Teens. Your Teen Mag.

https://yourteenmag.com/family-life/communication/how-to-start-good-habits

A Beginner's Guide to Goal Setting for Teens. (2020, May 13). Powerful Youth. https://powerfulyouth.com/beginners-guide-goal-setting-for-teens-smart-goals/

Help Unmotivated Teen Develop Long-term Goals. (2016, August 7). Intensive Care for You. https://intensivecareforyou.com/help-an-unmotivated-teen-make-long-term-goals/

Rippey, P. M.D. (2022.) Teenagers: How to Stay Healthy. FamilyDoctor.Org *https://familydoctor.org/https-familydoctor-org-teenagers-how-to-stay-healthy/*

Lee, A.M.I. (n.d.) Why Kids Struggle With Organization Skills. Www.understood.org. https://www.understood.org/en/articles/organization-challenges-in-children

Meldrum, A. (2020, May 6). 5 Overlooked Organizing Strategies For Teens - Made For Math. https://madeformath.com/organization/

<u>Other Books by Jessica L. Stevenson</u>

Step-by-Step Guide For First-Time Parents - Helpful Tips for Ages 0–3 Years: From Feeding Your Newborn to Potty Training a Toddler and a Lot More!

Click the link below to find out more!
https://www.amazon.com/dp/B09FF4P4B9

Positive Parenting – A Guide To Raising Happy Teens: How to Communicate and Live With Your Teens

Click the link below to find out more!
https://www.amazon.com/dp/B09JYP431B

Positive Minds – A Step-By-Step Guide To Mental Wellness For Children

Click the link below to find out more!
https://www.amazon.com/dp/B09Y2F9G8B

A Practical Guide to Adult Parenting – A Stress-Free Approach on How to Support, Motivate, and Adapt with your Grown-Up Kids

Click the link below to find out more!

https://www.amazon.com/dp/B0BZRZ34T4

Follow us on Facebook and Instagram for more useful parenting tips!

https://www.facebook.com/StepbyStep-Guide-For-FirstTime-Parents-223489799660552

https://www.instagram.com/parentingtips_jessica/